Mus

Christian

Toni Sherrington

BookLeaf
Publishing

Presentation by *BookLeaf Publishing*

Web: www.bookleafpub.com

E-mail: info@bookleafpub.com

ISBN: 9789357614948

First edition 2023

ACKNOWLEDGEMENT

Firstly, I want to thank my husband, Daniel, and my Mum and Dad, Elaine and John. Without all your love and support, I would have never become the person I am today. Your encouragement to keep going and follow God, wherever He leads, is something I truly cherish. I can never thank you enough for all that you do and you all mean the world to me. This book is for you.

Thanks also to all my other friends and family, including my foster families, for their amazing encouragement over the years. A particular thanks to Heather and Terry, who loved me when I was an angry and confused little girl and showed me the love of my eternal Heavenly Father. I also particularly want to thank the one who started off my love of poetry. Judy, without you, this book, and my poet heart, would have never been born.

Lastly, and most importantly, a massive thank you to God, whose steadfast love never fails!

PREFACE

I wrote my first poem when I was just 8 years old while I was in foster care. Entitled 'Winter Days', it was my first time attempting a poem... and a rhyming one at that! From that moment, my love of poetry and my psalmist anointing was born. Many friends and family can attest to my little poems that frequent birthday or Christmas cards or for other special occasions. This little collection is just that, a relatively random assortment of poems, some rhyming, some not, some are based on Bible verses, some on stories, but all written with a prayerful heart and God within them. With some poems, there's even something in the structure of how the poem looks, so keep an eye out for that too!

Psalm 91 is a very special Psalm for me and has kept me feeling safe and confident through all of life's ups and downs to this point. May you be blessed as you read my collection of Psalms and poems and who knows, maybe you'll feel inspired to write a little poem in a friend's card next time!

A Christmas Blessing

Another year has come and gone,
And what a year it's been;
Full of lots of ups and downs
And some bits in between.

This Christmas, this poem comes,
From our family to you,
To wish you love, peace and joy
This day and all year through.

May your life be full of love,
May your home be full of peace,
May your heart be full of joy,
May all your fear now cease.

May your family be full of health,
May you have no strife,
May you know God's blessing
In every part of life.

May you remember, at this time,
The reason for the gifts,
The reason for the lights,
And may it, your spirit, lift.

Today we celebrate the birth of Christ,
Who came from God above,
A God who brings peace and joy,
Whose very being is love.

This God who loves you so much,
 He sent His only Son
To take the blame for everything,
For all the bad you've done.

All it takes is you to ask
And he'll take it, big or small.
There is no sin that is too great;
His gift covers it all.

So to conclude, please hear my heart,
Read this and be blessed:
May your Christmas this year be joyful
And next year just the best.

On the birth of a baby

Congratulations from us to you
As you celebrate new birth!
May you enjoy each moment and
On waves of happiness surf.

What a wonderful occasion
To celebrate new life,
To thank God for bringing you all
Safely through the strife.

We pray that all goes well with you
As your family now expands,
As your love grows new feet
And chubby little hands.

We pray you're filled with energy
And that your little one sleeps.
We pray also for your marriage
And that patience you will keep.

So God bless your family,
And as your little one grows,
May they know God's love and peace
Wheresoever they go.

A Child of God (1 John 3)

Oh what kind of love you have
To call us daughter and son,
To adopt us into your family,
To call us one by one.

You call us your children,
For that is what we are.
You lavish your love upon us
Whether we're near or far.

It is quite a miracle
That you, so much, care
That you sent your son from Heaven
So we can meet you there.

As much as a parent loves a child
They'd sacrifice it all,
Your love for us is even greater
Despite how far we fall.

You would leave the 99
The one to chase after.
Through Jesus' teachings, you show us how
You love us as a Father.

We just have to receive you,
Open the doors inside,
Let your love and light flow in,
Like a gentle, powerful tide.

So receive God's gift today,
Let Him take away your sin,
Come into His family,
Let Love welcome you in.

Baptism Reflection

I remember choosing God,
To follow Him all my days.
I remember choosing Love
And following His ways.

He commands us in the Bible,
Following our belief,
To be baptised in His name,
As we turn over a new leaf.

I remember the day all too well,
A special day for all,
When we celebrate Jesus' resurrection,
His victory over the fall.

Getting into the warm water of
A little baptismal pool,
I remember being asked
If I'd give Jesus my all.

As I said yes, the pastor smiled
And looked at me with love
And said he would baptise me
In the name of God above.

Falling back into the water,
I couldn't hear a sound.
It truly felt, for a moment, like
I was buried in the ground.

But then up, in Jesus' power,
I rose from the grave,
Washed clean with His blood and water
My life once again now saved.

It's been a few years since that time,
And life continues to expand,
But still I know, as I knew then,
My life is in His hand.

The Cathedral at Monreale

Surrounded by beauty, standing here,
Your powerful presence, loud and clear.
The bustle of the city now so faint
As I take in mosaic, stained glass and paint.
A wonderful cathedral on hallowed ground.
I dare not talk, not even a sound.
There's a hush in here, despite the crowd,
Even my friends, so raucous and loud,
Can't help but be in silent awe
As I quietly contemplate the work of the Lord.
It's here displayed on all the walls
The Bible stories that started it all.
From the beginning of time, to Jesus, God's Son,
Then onto depicting when God's work is done.
Stories full of intricate detail,
All shown in mosaic, a beautiful tale.

The Lord's Table

A simple meal at this table,
Just some wine and bread,
A strange custom, from outside,
Given by one who's dead.

But Jesus isn't gone,
He's gifted us with life,
Eternal life in Heaven
Free of sin and strife.

This meal serves to remind us,
That he gave up everything
So we could be freed from all guilt
And shame that's caused by sin.

Not just freedom though,
Does this simple meal proclaim,
It draws us all together
As one, in Jesus' name.

For we are a family,
Though many, we are one
Brought together by one God,
Father, Spirit, Son.

Such a simple meal,
A little bread and wine,
But I belong to Jesus
And Jesus now is mine.

John 3:16

God created the world
Ordered all creation yet
Died upon a cross.

Love like His is all-encompassing and
Overwhelms everything in its path.
Verily, I tell you, Jesus gave
Everything that you might be saved from
Death.

We cannot comprehend
Or even begin to understand the
Real, amazing love of God,
Laid out on a cross,
Displayed for all to see.

God sent His Son down to Earth,
All humanity to save in a
Very painful death
Even though He is God.

So that he could return us to Himself,
Outside the tomb, women found Jesus,
Not where he was laid

But alive.
Everlasting life is what Jesus offers.
Let Him in,
Into your heart,
Even the bits that are
Very dark
Even the bits that are
Shameful

Even the bits that are
Terrible
Even the bits that are
Rageful.
Nothing is too bad for Him.
All He wants is to
Lavish His unending

Love upon you and welcome you
Into His family and into Heaven,
Forgiveness given and life
Everlasting.

Wedding Day Blessing

A blessing's contained in this poem
From me to both of you,
As you start on this marriage journey,
Made for just two.

May you have patience with each other
As you grow and learn.
May you find joy in small things
And for comfort, to each other, turn.

May you know God's presence
Every single day
As, together, you walk and learn
All along life's way.

May you have many years and
May you have lots of fun
As you discover what it's like
To have a special one.

May God bless your family
As it is in His will,
Whether it be big or small,
I pray He's in the centre still.

May your home be filled with love,
Lots of peace and laughter.
May you be so very content and
Live happily ever after.

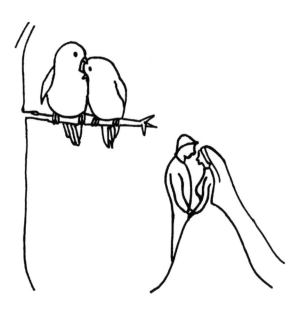

Psalm of Praise

How marvellous is our God!
All his plans work toward our good
Loving us as only He could.
Life is ours because He's our father
Everlasting in Heaven, ever after.
Lord you're amazing and so kind
Uplifting spirits and fears you bind
Just because you love us so much
Awesome is your powerful touch.
How marvellous is our God!

First Home Blessing

This poem contains a blessing,
From us both to you,
As you've moved into your home,
So lovely and so new.

Your first home together,
Or at least the first you own;
May your love for each other grow
As new seeds are sown.

May your home see lots of laughter
And bring comfort when you're sad;
May your marriage be much strengthened
Through good times and bad.

May your home be full of peace;
May it bring you lots of joy;
May it hear the pitter-patter of little feet
Whether furry, or girl, or boy.

May your work be blessed,
So too your times of play;
May you grow closer to our God
As you praise and pray.

May you be filled with energy and
May you, when needed, rest.
So may your life be fruitful,
And may your home be blessed.

Seaside Reflection

I stand there on the beach.
To some people this is just a beach,
Of hard pebbles, rough water, ragged cliffs.
It's impossible to swim there so it's often very
quiet, only fishermen and their boats keeping
the sea company with the occasional
dog walker going off on a romp.
But it isn't plain or boring.
Just looking around
I see things,
things that remind me
of the God I serve and love
and of the life He has given me
and called me to. To think that He created
this and He created me takes my breath away.
I look at these hard pebbles which others say are
a nuisance and are not as good as the soft sand.
They are a magnificent array of different
colours,
different shapes and sizes and textures.
And yet all serve one purpose.
As I look down at one
I notice something.
It is smooth and rounded
having been bounced for miles along

the uneven sea bed, its edges worn away and
its surface polished to a gentle curving dome.
Lying at my feet were two stones that I had to
pick up; heart-shaped and lying side by side.
"I love you, my child," says my Father to me
and I feel the wind, which can be wild,
gently caress my skin, holding me
in an embrace with Him.
Playing with a dog in the shallows
further along the beach were children
laughing with joy as the waves crashed
and the wind danced around them, tossing hair
and clothing everywhere. Jesus said that
we should be as children and
these children were delighting themselves
in the sea and the nature that surrounded them.
Standing near me were some fishermen
seeing to their trawlers and their nets.
it's funny how for them the sea
provides food and
money
and yet can
just as easily remove
the fish, their livelihood,
their boats and their lives
with its enormous strength,
almighty power and the forceful spring tides.
For the sea is powerful.
Those who claim how gentle

the sea do not see just how mighty
it can be for water is gentle but when its wrath
is awakened, all can perish. The power of
the sea is demonstrated all around me. The
stones which have been dragged along the sea
bed and dumped in huge piles show its power.
The cliffs and rocks, immovable some might
say, crumble
against the force of the waves.
We say how desirable
a sea view
is
but when
the cliffs fall,
when the water
collapses them, it does not
discriminate and takes houses down.
Only a foolish man would build his house
on the sand or near the beach, those who are
wise keep well away from the cliff edge or the
sea shore.
Foolish men try and stop the sea.
They use their defences
sea walls, banks, groins
to try and keep it there,
keep it at bay out of the
town. They try to protect
lives and homes they say.
This thing will hold better

the sea can be contained
the sea's power drained.
After all the sea is not as
powerful as we are; no
nothing is as powerful
as us as we are in control.
But pray who can defeat
something so powerful
that it can rip through anything in its path!
God.

In the Woods

As I stand here, under the trees,
I hear the wind whisper through the leaves,
The sunlight dapples on the ground
Shafts of sunbeam all around.
A carpet of bluebells coats the soil,
As a squirrel hurries home, carrying its spoil.
A rabbit hops by, with four kits in tow,
And nearby walking, a stag and a doe.
All around me are signs that Spring's in the air,
Here in the woods, I can't help but stare
At the nature surrounding me Father God made,
Before the sunlight does start to fade.

Darkness falls quickly here in the wood,
And creatures head home, as I now should.
But I linger awhile as day turns to night,
While it's difficult to see, what a remarkable
sight!
An owl swoops by, looking for prey,
As bats dance in the air at the end of the day.
A fox slopes by, heading home to its den
All nature wary to the sounds of men.
I thank God for this time, here in the wood,
As He allowed me to see the world be as it
should.

Nature in harmony, a peaceful time,
As I sit here, to write my own little rhyme.

So get out, take a walk, see the woods for
yourself.
Be still, be quiet, leave your games on the shelf.
Spend time in prayer out on nature's ground,
For here, the works of God's hands can be found.
And if you listen, without making a noise,
You're more likely to hear that still, small voice.

Psalm of Peace

For peace, Lord Jesus, thank you.

When all seems chaos
And all seems lost,
All seems confused
And turned about,

For peace, Lord Jesus, thank you.

When life seems like a stormy sea
And we are, but a minute from drowning,
When life seems to suffocate
And all colours turn to grey,

For peace, Lord Jesus, thank you.

When everything seems hopeless
And we are in the darkest pit,
When despair threatens
And depression hits,

For peace, Lord Jesus, thank you.

Even when we can't feel it,
Even when we do things wrong,
Or we don't do
That which we should,
For peace, Lord Jesus, thank you.

When the world won't stop spinning,
Like a carousel, out of control,
Life a flying rollercoaster,
Upside-down and inside-out,

For peace, Lord Jesus, thank you.

We remember that you wept,
We remember that you struggled,
You suffered for everything we do,
In that, we can take comfort.

For peace, Lord Jesus, thank you.

A Birthday blessing

A birthday blessing today is sent
From me to you.
I hope today is all you want
And all your dreams come true.

As you get one year older,
And celebrate who you are,
Give thanks to God for all He's given
Throughout life so far.

Whether you are young or old,
Having a party or getting a gift,
Remember God's faithfulness
And may it, your Spirit, lift.

May this next age bring you joy
May it be full of peace and love,
May you know the Spirit's gifts,
May you feel blessed by God above.

May you enjoy today
Whatsoever it brings,
So have a happy birthday
Full of amazing things.

But please also remember
And don't lose sight of this,
Today, we celebrate who you are,
But forever, you are His.

A Time of Confusion

O Lord, all is confusion around me.
Help me, Lord.
I thought I knew the way you were pointing,
The way to go,
But nothing is happening the way I thought.
What to do now?
Like a small boat, being tossed around,
This way and that,
Where up is down and left is right.
Nothing seems certain,
Nothing seems like sure ground and no water
seems safe.
Dropping anchor?
Mine had no effect as the waves overpowered it.
A safe harbour?
I can't see through the storm to find one.
What to do?
The waves are climbing higher and threatening
to overwhelm my small craft.
Pray, girl, pray.
There is one safe harbour, one solid rock.
Jesus.
One can calm the water,
Only one who knows the way,
One who can provide the map,

One who knows the end
From the beginning,
Who knows
Everything,
Who isn't confused,
Who is not flummoxed,
Whose steps are certain,
Who's faithful to all He promised.
Trust in Him to show you your path.
Trust Him to guide your steps.
When all seems confused,
He is not a God of confusion,
He is the Alpha and
The Omega, the
First and Last.
For He is
Love.

Psalm of Lament

Father God, I cry out to you.
I feel lost as one in a maze with no direction.
I feel as though a light has gone out and all is dim
and dark.
Help me, Lord Jesus, I pray.
Teach me and show me how to live according to your
ways.
Save me from the darkness surrounding me.
Come to me, Holy Spirit.
Flood the world with your light.
Let me feel again your warm embrace.
Fill my world with your colour and guide my steps.
Lord God, your will in my life.

On the death of a loved one

I pray you'll know God's comfort.
I pray He helps you to go on.
I pray you'll feel His arms around you,
As you grieve your one now gone.

I hold you tightly in my heart,
You're in every thought and prayer,
If there's something, anything, I can do
Just call and I'll be there.

I know right now it feels so raw,
As though tears are without end,
But take some comfort, find some joy
That you'll see them once again.

Jeremiah 29:11

You know the plans you have for us,
Which we cannot begin to see,
Plans to prosper, not to harm,
To make me a better me.

You are always working for my good;
You know me inside out,
You knew before the world was born
That I would come about.

I know you aren't pacing up in Heaven
Wringing out your hands,
Wondering how on earth this happened:
It was in your plans.

For you can turn all things round
So they work out for the best;
No circumstances are too bad that
Through them, I can't be blessed.

So even when life seems tough
And I feel it's gone awry,
I know that I can lean on you
The ultimate, powerful ally.

I can trust you have a plan
And that plan is something great;
I pray that if I wander off
You will set me straight.

So Lord, I commit my life to you,
I entrust me to your care,
For you know the plans you have for me,
And you will always be there.